ONE DAY

A STORY ABOUT Positive Attitude

To Josh
Dana & Hugo

First published by Nanshe Publishing in 2015
Nanshe Publishing
PO Box 20111 Pioneer Park
123 Pioneer Drive
Kitchener ON
N2P 1L9

Copyright © Nanshe Publishing 2015

Written by Barb Chrysler www.barbchrysler.biz
Edited by Ella Marie Wilson & Alex Craig
Illustrated & Designed by Philip McIvor www.hpmcivor@mac.com

For every 500 books printed 30 trees have been donated to Tree Canada for reforestation in areas most needed

All rights reserved. No part of this publication may be reproduced, stored in a retrieval system or transmitted, in any form or by any means, electronic, mechanical, photocopying, recording or otherwise, without the prior permission of the copyright holder.

ISBN number 978-0-9948049-0-7

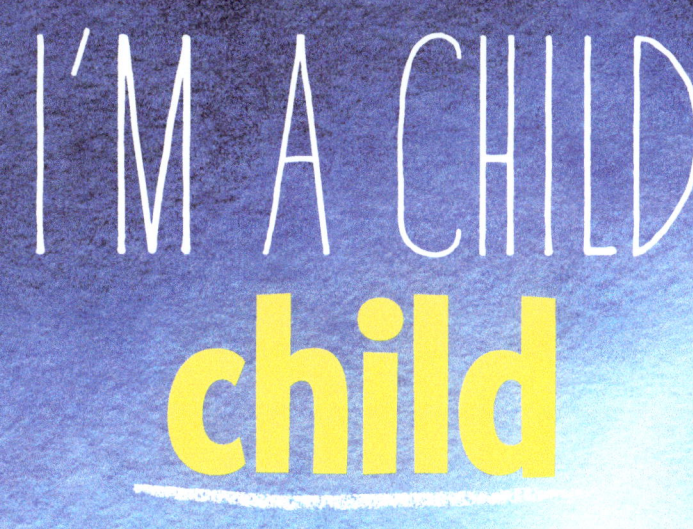

I **work hard** TO **IMPROVE,** EVEN WHEN **no one is watching** LIKE **MIA** HAMM

I **eat well** AND **FOCUS** ON **FITNESS** ‹LIKE› **ABBY** WAMBACH

play FAIR

LIKE

DAVID ALABA

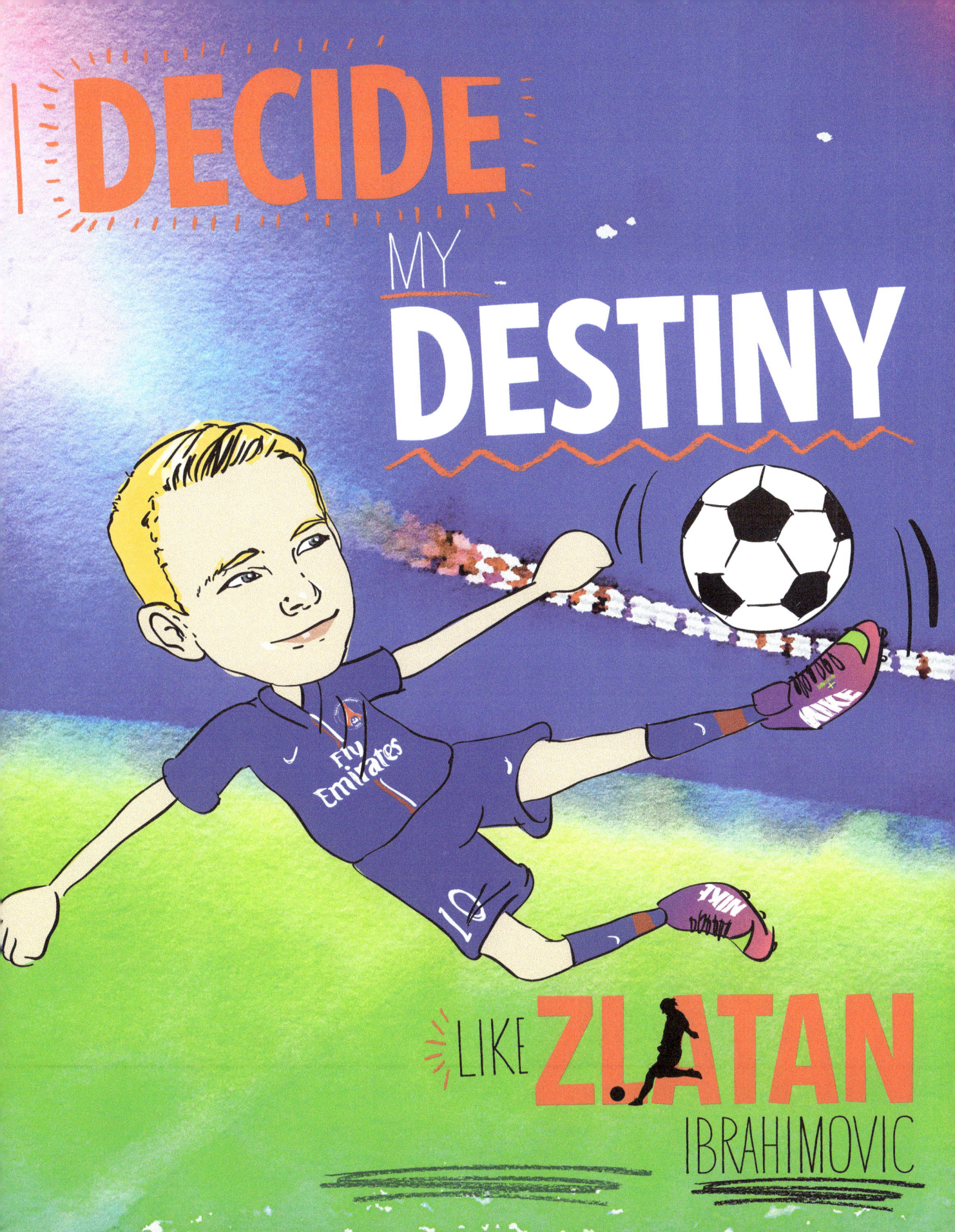

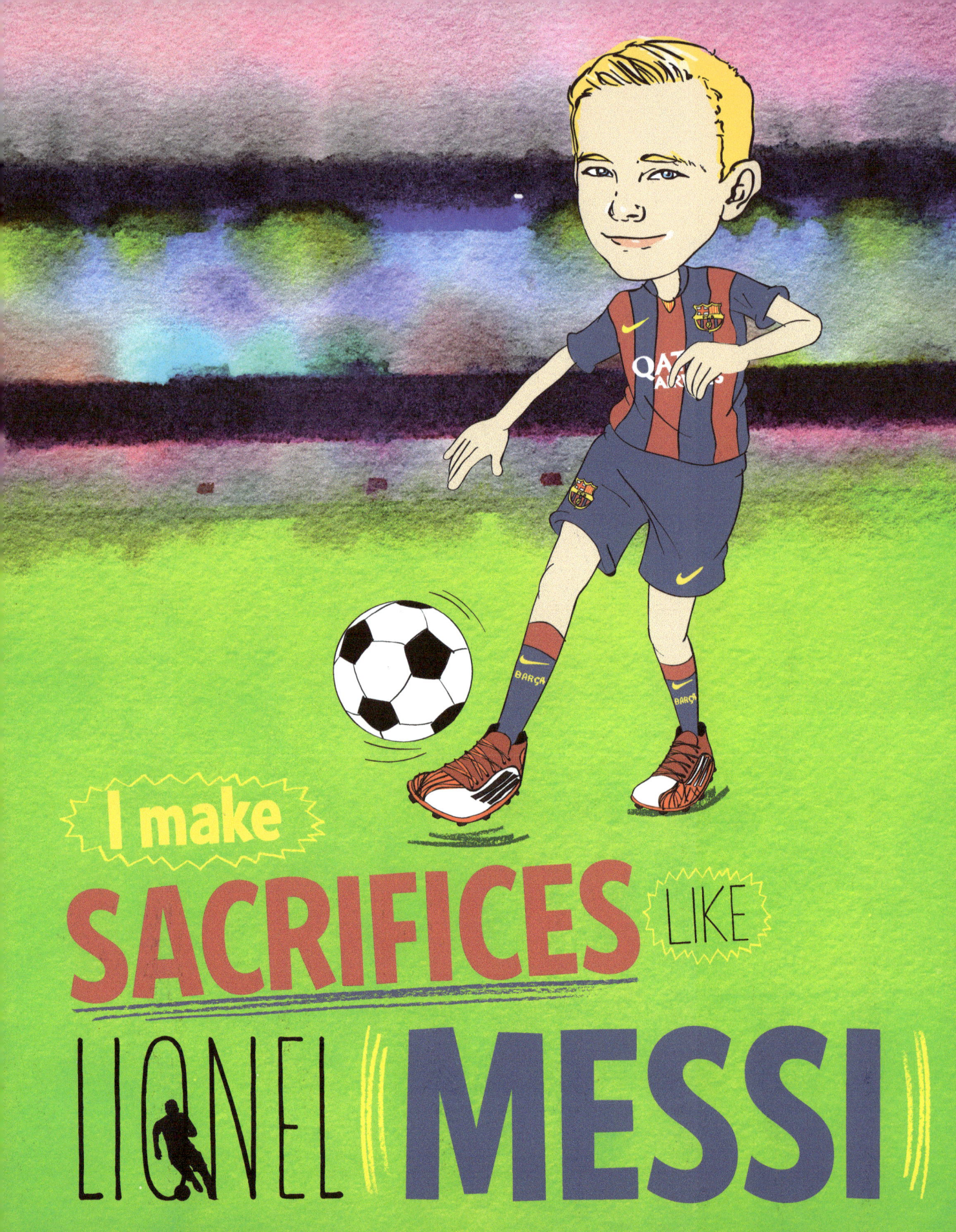

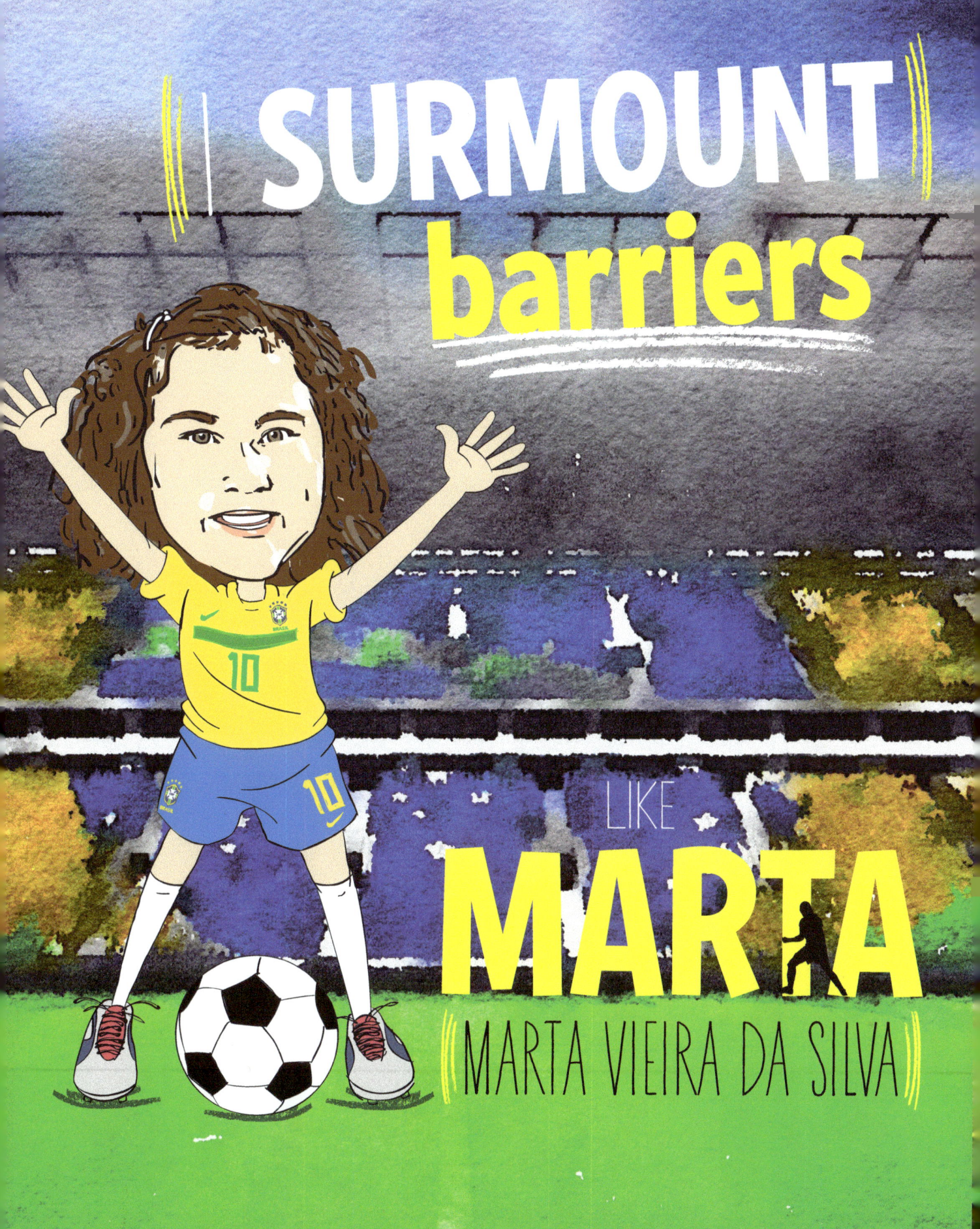

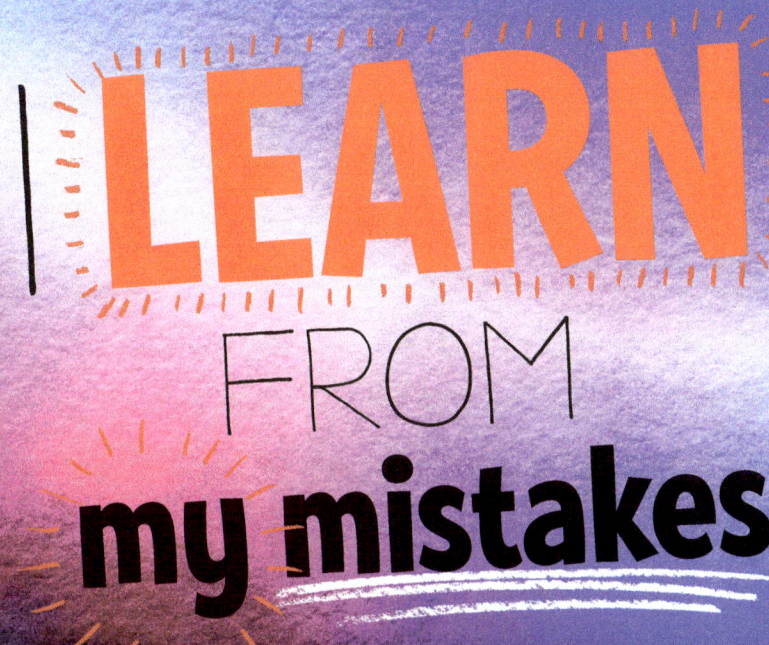

PELÉ HAD A DREAM

Pelé, originally named Edson Arantes do Nascimento, grew up poor in Brazil. He had no shoes, no soccer balls, no organized soccer team to play for, and was often hungry. Despite these barriers, when he was about 9 years old, he told his dad he would win the World Cup. He let nothing keep him from his desire to play soccer and found a solution for every problem life put in front of him. To solve the challenge of not having a ball he made one out of socks and newspapers. Later he set up a team on his own by gathering together a group of friends. Then, to get a real ball, they began selling peanuts to raise enough money to buy one. They played without shoes in the street. When he became good enough, many teams wanted him to play for them. He was hired by Santos FC, when he was only 15, and went on to play for Brazil, winning the World Cup three times. Many regard him as the greatest player who has ever lived.

CRISTIANO RONALDO BELIEVES IN HIMSELF

Cristiano Ronaldo was born in Portugal, and as a child, his life was challenging. His father drank too much, his mother had to work long hours, and he was kicked out of school when he was 14 years old. His mother encouraged him to chase his football dream. At one time, Ronaldo was thought to be too small by his coaches at the Sporting Youth Academy. But this didn't stop him, and he continued to practice his ball control and weight training. He believed in his ability to be the best soccer player, and to this day still works hard to achieve this. His coaches have said he is tireless and never gives up. He has won many awards, including three Ballon d'Ors, as well as numerous other trophies. Having scored over 50 international goals, he is Portugal's best striker of all time.

LIONEL MESSI MAKES SACRIFICES

Lionel Messi was born in Argentina. He was noticeably smaller than other children, and was diagnosed with a growth hormone deficiency. FC Barcelona Youth Academy offered to pay for medication to help this condition, which his mom and dad could not afford. His whole family sacrificed so that Messi could pursue his dream. They all hoped he would grow tall enough to play professional football. The family moved to Barcelona, Spain, when Messi was 13 years old, and he was often homesick for the country he left behind. However, he worked hard, and grew to 5'7". He has had a phenomenally successful career with Barcelona. In four consecutive Champions League competitions he was the top scorer, and led his country in the 2014 World Cup Final. He has won numerous trophies, including four Ballon d'Ors.

ABBY WAMBACH EATS WELL AND FOCUSES ON FITNESS

Abby Wambach is regarded as one of the best female soccer players ever. Having scored 182 times for the US team, she holds the record for the greatest number of international goals scored by any player, male or female. In addition, she has won numerous awards including the 2012 FIFA World Player of the Year, which made her the first American to receive the trophy. At a young age she was playing for a girls recreational soccer team, and after she scored 27 goals in 3 games, they moved her to a boys league. She believes that it is important to eat better than others and to focus on your fitness in order to achieve success.

MIA HAMM WORKS HARD TO IMPROVE EVEN WHEN NO ONE IS WATCHING

Mia Hamm was born with a clubfoot and needed corrective shoes. Once she was out of braces there was no stopping her. Inspired by her brother she began to play soccer. She looked up to her brother and was devastated when he died at an early age from a rare blood disease. Mia found soccer helpful in dealing with her grief. Her father was in the military, and because of that, she moved many times. She often played on boys' teams. For the majority of her career there were no professional womens' soccer leagues, however when a league was established in 2001, she was able to play for three years for the Washington Freedom FC. She also played on Olympic teams that won two Gold medals and one Silver medal. Mia believes it is important to have drive and determination, to push beyond your limits, and to put in more hours of training than other people. Mia is considered one of the best female players of all time.

GEORGE WEAH HAS FAITH

George Weah was born in the slums of Africa and raised by his grandmother after his parents separated. It was a very poor area and the neighbours often fed George, because his family didn't have enough food. As a child, he played soccer with makeshift balls and tin cans, but George dreamt of playing football, and scoring goals, and his great uncle believed that God had a destiny for him that he had to follow. Most of the men in the neighbourhood, where he grew up, did not have jobs. Yet George had faith in his ability and began playing in the Liberian domestic league in his early teens. When he was 22 years old, he was signed to play professionally in Europe. In 2004, he was voted by the world's top sports journalists as African Player of the Century. He contributed his own money to sponsor the Liberian National Team, which he played for and managed, scoring 13 goals before his retirement. George is grateful for the opportunities that his talent and hard work have provided him with: "Today I'm sitting at my pool when before I never even had room to sleep. I'm grateful to God and to football."

ZLATAN IBRAHIMOVIC DECIDES HIS DESTINY

Zlatan's parents were new immigrants to Sweden. His father and mother separated, and after living with his mother for a while, Zlatan went to stay with his father. His childhood was tough, as his mother would sometimes hit him, and his father drank a lot of alcohol. Sometimes Zlatan was hungry, but when he went to look for something to eat, there was only beer in the refrigerator and no food. This made him angry. One positive thing about his childhood was that there were football pitches in his neighbourhood, and he spent a lot of time playing outside. He loved soccer and sometimes, as a young boy, even slept with the ball, dreaming about the tricks he would perform the next day. His idol was the football star, Ronaldo, and he saw the Brazilian score two goals in a Milan stadium. This really inspired him and he told his coach that he too would play professional football one day. Zlatan believes he created his own destiny and overcame his circumstances to achieve professional success. He now plays as striker for Paris Saint-Germain, and has made over 100 appearances for Sweden. His fridge is always full of food.

DAVID BECKHAM OVERCOMES HARDSHIP

David Beckham was born in England. By the time he was 9 years of age he was determined to be a football player and believed it was possible for him to achieve this goal. He practiced hard, completely focused on his dream, and at the age of 14 signed a contract with Manchester United. While Beckham received a lot of honours, he made what he acknowledges was a huge mistake in kicking out at an opposing player in the 1998 World Cup. This resulted in him being sent off, and a penalty kick, which some attribute as the reason why England were knocked out of the competition. The fans began to bully him, and he sometimes even had to have police escort him to games. It was one of the most difficult times of his life. But he continued to play soccer, and to do his best. In 2002 he scored the winning goal from the penalty spot in England's World Cup victory against Argentina, and in doing so won back the support of fans. He has gone on to receive numerous awards and become one of the richest soccer celebrities.

NICO CALABRIA LETS NOTHING STOP HIM

Nico Calabria was born with one leg, but this has never stopped him from achieving his goals. By the age of 5, he was playing soccer on a regular team. He soon became one of the youngest players to be selected for the US National Amputee squad. In his first National Team game, he scored a goal against Mexico to achieve a 2-1 win. He is very appreciative of his parents support. In addition to achieving his soccer dream, he was also the youngest person to ever reach the summit of Mount Kilimanjaro on crutches, and in doing so raised over $100,000 for the Free Wheelchair Mission, which provides wheelchairs at no cost to people in the developing world. He lets nothing stop him from accomplishing his dreams.

MARTA OVERCOMES BARRIERS

Marta Vieira da Silva had no female role models, and there were no local teams for girls that she could play on. Soccer was not a sport played by many women in Brazil, yet she pursued her dream of becoming a professional footballer. Her ambition was to compete as part of Brazil's women's team against other countries. She first realized her own potential when she stood out as a top player in the boys' teams that she was playing on. Then, at 14 years old, she took a three-day trip to Rio de Janeiro to try out for the top women's team. Successful, she never returned home, and quit school to pursue her dream of a career in sport. When asked if she was scared to leave home and move to Rio, she replied: "Why would I be scared? It was in my character to want to achieve my goal, and that was where my goal was. So I had to go there." She is now considered to be one of the best female soccer players of all time, and has competed for Brazil in three FIFA Women's World Cups.

MICHELLE AKERS PRACTICES THINGS SHE DOES NOT ENJOY AND FEARS

Michelle Akers started her international career in 1985 and scored fifteen goals for the US team in just twenty-four matches. Despite suffering from chronic fatigue syndrome, she worked ferociously hard on her game and led her national team to success in the 1991 and 1999 Women's World Cups. Michelle is one of the great international soccer players of all time and was honoured by inclusion in the National Soccer Hall of Fame. She was recognized by FIFA in 2000, jointly with Chinese star, Sun Wen, as Female Player of the Century. Michelle has said that players have a tendency to practice what they like and what they are good at. She believes, however, that it is important to practice what you are not good at and fear.

DAVID ALABA PLAYS FAIR

David Alaba was born in Austria. He plays, as left-back, for Bayern Munich, and since the age of 17, for the Austria national football team. During his football career, David has had to overcome many challenges, resulting from injuries and racism. Despite all these obstacles, David has developed a reputation for consistently playing fair. Red and yellow cards are given to players by the referee when they commit fouls, and most defenders receive these penalties sometimes. However, David has not received a single card in the last two seasons, and only one yellow card in the season before. In 2011, when he was just 19, he was recognized as Austrian Footballer of the Year.

HOPE SOLO LEARNS FROM HER MISTAKES

America's famous goalkeeper, Hope Solo, learned how to play soccer from her father. In high school, she was a forward who scored a lot of goals; However, at university, with encouragement from her coach, she learned to become a goalkeeper. Her level of commitment and solid self-belief led her to be recognized as one of the best goalies in the world. She has made mistakes in her life that even, on one occasion, led her to be suspended from the team for 30 days. But she has learned from these mistakes. She now has this advice for younger players: "You may have made a big mistake and may have made a bad decision, and you pay the consequences for them, but you don't just give up. You keep going. And you learn from your mistakes."

PHILIPP LAHM IS A TEAM PLAYER

Philipp Lahm has dreamed about winning the World Cup since he was a kid; a goal he would one day achieve. Now, he has captained both Bayern Munich and the German national team. Considered one of the best fullbacks in the world, you can imagine his surprise when his coach wanted him to play in the midfield position, a change many players would not have relished. However, he listened to his coach, asked questions, discussed the idea, and successfully made the necessary transition. In one game, he made 134 passes with a 100% completion rate. Philipp does what is right for the team; he is a team player.

RONALDO OVERCOMES CHALLENGES

Ronaldo Luís Nazário de Lima, famous across the world simply as "Ronaldo," was born in Brazil and grew up in a poor neighbourhood. His talent for sports was noticed from an early age, and by the time he was 16 years old, he had been selected for the Cruzeiro team. As a professional, he suffered a severe knee injury, which forced him to undergo surgery. Because of the recovery period required he wasn't able to return to football for about two years. But the injury and pain didn't stop this top player from making a comeback and scoring goals. Ronaldo has said that it was his passion and love of soccer that kept him going through the sacrifices needed to recover from the knee surgery. He has played in two winning Brazil teams at FIFA World Cups, and is recognized as one of the Greatest Players of the 20th Century by World Soccer.

MANUEL NEUER HAS A POSITIVE ATTITUDE

Manuel Neuer was born in West Germany. He plays goalie for Bayern Munich and for the German national team. In 2014, he was awarded the Golden Glove for his performance in the FIFA World Cup. He had achieved over 1000 sequential minutes in the competition without conceding a goal. Manuel takes care of his health and continues to work on his skills. But he says the most important part of a successful performance is the mental game. He said: "I do not think negatively. I always think positive. If you ponder all the time about what is or could be dangerous, it would kill all the fun." In 2014 he was voted the world's best goalkeeper.

ARJEN ROBBEN MAKES THE BEST OF LIFE

Arjen Robben is from the Netherlands and plays for the national team and for Bayern Munich. In 2012 he missed two penalty kicks and suffered an injury, which resulted in him losing his place as first choice striker. However, he never gave up, and in 2013 he had what many think was his finest season, scoring 21 goals and 17 assists. His achievements and come back are thought to be the result of his attitude. During this time on the substitutes' bench he increased his efforts, training even harder at the gym. At 31 years old, he is ranked as one of the top three players in the world, and still appears to be only increasing his level of performance. Arjen Robben is a player who makes the best of what life gives him.

ALEX MORGAN BELIEVES IN THE POWER OF CONFIDENCE

Alex Morgan played many sports when she was young and didn't start playing soccer until she was 14 years old. Yet she was a first draft pick in 2011, and the youngest player on the US team for the FIFA Women's World Cup. In 2012, she was part of the team that won a gold medal at the London Olympics. Alex credits soccer with giving her confidence. Every time she joined a new team she had self-doubt, and this forced her to work through her insecurities. She wrote a series of books called "The Kicks" to help show young girls the importance of confidence. She said: "It is important that, as women, we stand up for ourselves, stand up for our peers, and show the power that confidence can have for women everywhere."

ZINEDINE ZIDANE HELPS PEOPLE LESS FORTUNATE

Zinedine Zidane was born in France, after his mother and father had emigrated from Algeria. They lived in a tough neighbourhood, and his parents struggled to find work. Zidane began playing soccer early, and has achieved a huge amount with clubs from across Europe, especially Juventus and Real Madrid. In 1998 he was man of the match in the World Cup final, and he is now assistant coach for Real Madrid. He has a big heart and does a lot of charity work, regularly taking part in the United Nations "Match Against Poverty," and fulfilling his role as a United Nations Goodwill Ambassador since 2001. "We should not be deterred," he says, "by the magnitude of remaining problems because the good news is that each of us can do something to help reduce poverty."

Positive Inspiration

The players mentioned within this story are only some of the many within the sport of football who have shown a positive attitude. There is a lot that we can learn from reading about high achievers and how they accomplish their goals.

REFERENCES FOR QUOTES

CNN. (2013). Olympian Alex Morgan's Message to Girls: Confidence in Face of Challenges. Retrieved May 31, 2015. http://www.cnn.com/2013/06/13/world/girl-rising-alex-morgan/

Sokolove, M. (2009). Kicking Off. The New York Times. Retrieved May 31 2015. http://www.nytimes.com/2009/04/05/magazine/05marta-t.html?pagewanted=all&_r=0

Solo, H. Hope Solo Website. Retrieved May 31, 2015.

Gala Magazine. (2014). Interview with Manuel Neuer in Gala Magazine. Manuel Neuer. Retrieved May 31, 2015. http://melanie-hh.tumblr.com/post/105461995980/interview-with-manuel-neuer-in-gala-men-magazine

Trans World International/IMB Media. (August, 2010). George Weah – Part 2. Retrieved May 31. 2015. https://www.youtube.com/watch?v=SUINYqGEbhO

United Nations Information Service Vienna. (March, 2001). French Soccer Champion Zinedine Zidane to Be Appointed (Press release). Retrieved May 31, 2015. http://www.unis.unvienna.org/unis/pressrels/2001/note126.html

www.ingramcontent.com/pod-product-compliance
Lightning Source LLC
Chambersburg PA
CBHW061932290426

44113CB00024B/2892